HEALING MINISTRY &
PASTORAL PRAYER
MINISTRY

An Introduction
for the Local Church

David Pytches

NEW WINE INTERNATIONAL PUBLISHING

HEALING MINISTRY AND PASTORAL PRAYER MINISTRY: AN INTRODUCTION FOR THE LOCAL CHURCH

PUBLISHED BY   New Wine International Publishing
                4A Ridley Avenue, Ealing, London W13 9XW
ISBN 1 902977 01 7
© David Pytches/New Wine
First Published November 1987
This edition July 1999

INTRODUCTION

John Wimber, with his team, first visited St. Andrew's, Chorleywood, in 1981. We witnessed four significant things. One: Effective *healings*. Two: Release of the healing ministry to the *laity*. Three: Our dependence upon the *Holy Spirit* in healing. Four: This ministry could be operated in a traditional church like the Church of England.

Following John Wimber's model we began to develop this healing ministry along the lines spelt out in this little booklet. Now, due to an on-going demand we are re-publishing the material under New Wine International. Many busy church leaders feel the need for such a ministry in their churches but, just as we did, they are looking for help in setting it up. They neither have the time nor the desire to re-create the wheel and are glad to take over something which others have taught and tested and that is what we have been doing over the years. We have continued to teach and minister along these lines at our New Wine Conferences. We trust and pray that many new leaders may find these guidelines helpful also.

Yours sincerely
David Pytches
1999

Acknowledgements
All scripture quotations are taken from the Holy Bible, New International Version, ©1973, 1978, 1984 by International Bible Society. used by permission of Hodder and Stoughton Limited. All rights reserved.

HEALING MINISTRY AND PASTORAL PRAYER MINISTRY: AN INTRODUCTION FOR THE LOCAL CHURCH

DEFINITIONS

Healing Ministry Training

The term 'Healing Ministry Training' has been used to cover the prayer ministry which is offered at after-service time of prayer and in Home or Bible Study Groups.

Pastoral Prayer Ministry Training

The Pastoral Prayer Ministry, defined in the past as **Prayer Counselling,** covers the deeper needs of individuals within the fellowship. These should be addressed outside the context of the after-service ministry. We believe the new title is appropriate for a resource which is offered as part of overall pastoral support.

FOUNDATIONS OF PASTORAL SUPPORT

Background

Friendship and small groups can provide the basis of gospel-based evangelism leading to invitations to guest services, socials, Alpha courses and other outreach events. Both the small groups and the church itself seek to provide a safe place where people can not only meet Christ as their personal Saviour but continue to mature as Christians. This growth, in the context of Christian fellowship, worship and teaching, may include the need to deal with unresolved past issues in the individual's life.

Leadership Role

The leadership is naturally involved in giving spiritual guidance, prayer and pastoral support in individual cases, but small group ministry, eg Home Groups and after-service prayer times, can also provide a safe place for individuals to deal with specific personal prayer needs.

Existing Pastoral Care

Many churches have a well-established pastoral oversight. The training and appointment of lay people will require some re-thinking about the exercise of authority. Delegation must be balanced with accountability to the leadership.

Problems may also arise from the tension between a commitment to confidentiality and the need for pastoral leaders to know what is going on. The individual receiving prayer may, at a later stage, confide in his or her pastoral leader. But no such confidences will be shared without the knowledge and consent of the one receiving ministry unless the individual is at personal risk or it is a matter which requires to be reported by law. (See Guidelines for Dealing with Child Abuse, pages 31, 32).

THE CHURCH'S COMMISSION

Christ's Commission

Christ's Commission to the Church is wide but contains biblical foundations which can guide us in our love and care of others. The ministry we follow we believe is biblical, Christ-centred and Holy Spirit-led and seeks to help people towards change and growth in every aspect of their lives.

Biblical Foundation

Matt 28:19	Go and make disciples of all nations, baptising them in the name of the Father, Son and Holy Spirit and teaching them to obey everything I have commanded you.
Luke 9:2	Among other things He sent them out to preach the Kingdom of God and to heal the sick, etc.
Luke 11:13	If you then, though you are evil, know how to give good gifts to your children, how much more will your Father in heaven give the Holy Spirit to those who ask him.
Jn 15:12	My command is this. Love one another as I have loved you.
Is 53:5	But He was pierced for our transgressions, He was crushed for our iniquities, the punishment that brought us peace was upon Him and by His wounds we are healed.
Is 61:	The anointing of the Lord was upon him to ... set captives free, bind up the broken-hearted ...

1 Pet 2:24	He Himself bore our sins in His body on the tree, so that we might die to sins and live for righteousness; by His wounds you have been healed.
Jn 8:31,32	If you hold to my teaching you are really my disciples. Then you will know the truth and the truth will set you free.
Rom 12:2	Do not conform any longer to the pattern of this world but be transformed by the renewing of your mind.

MINISTER'S RESPONSIBILITY

Leadership and Delegation

The leader, minister or pastor needs to 'own' this ministry – to initiate it and take responsibility for it. In practice he/she can not be deeply involved in the ministry itself, because of other responsibilities and duties. How the church responds depends greatly on whether the minister is willing to accept his/her leadership role; by example, and teaching, seeking to make the church a 'safe place'; and by releasing (ie, delegating) the ministry to trained and authorised lay people. In that, he/she needs to be a risk taker trusting in the Holy Spirit.

Teaching

The leader should make it his/her practice to teach into this area of ministry, both to the team and to the congregation as a whole. He should explain the work of the Holy Spirit within the overall ministry of the church and our need to learn to understand and follow what the Holy Spirit is doing.

Authority

The leader should initiate the ministry where it is not already exercised. He/she needs to be seen to be in authority, taking overall responsibility for the ministry even though not always directly involved; willing to give the major part, if not all, of the teaching himself; being seen as the one who authorises the individual members of the team; explains to the congregation as a whole what is happening, especially when anything out of the ordinary occurs; providing values and guidelines which are available to all for the ministry; and giving corrective guidance and discipline where this is necessary without public condemnation of individuals or general withdrawal of the ministry after initial mistakes. We all learn by our mistakes and can grow through them.

Dangers

Leaders may be in danger of falling into two traps:

Either – delegating and stepping back, ie, leaving everything to others. Here the ministry is not under his/her authority or blessing and it will wither (the leader must truly 'own' it);

Or – there can be over-involvement in which case the ministry will not mature and the minister's other responsibilities can suffer.

The Church as a Safe Place

We have often heard it being said, "I could not possibly share this with anyone in my own Church". The local church must work at establishing a reputation for being a safe place.

Values

The minister must teach and continue to teach the values which undergird the ministry. We suggest a summary which may be found on page 20.

Confidentiality

Lack of confidentiality can be seen as a significant barrier to individual willingness to respond to the work of the Holy Spirit.

We must, however, be vigilant about confidentiality in every aspect of this ministry, whether the sharing is something small or large, whether in a Home or Bible Study Group, at the prayer time after the service or in times of planned prayer ministry with a praying couple. Confidentiality is vital if we want this ministry to be safe for those who are making themselves so vulnerable to us in sharing themselves.

Ministers know this only too well but lay people need to be taught. The congregation, and in particular the ministry team, should be reminded of the importance of confidentiality and propriety, and the way they minister to each other. An important question will always be, "How would I like to be ministered to in this way?"

Training

Training is offered to anyone who wants to be involved in the Healing Ministry, although taking part in the training does not automatically mean that the individual will be authorised to minister. The leader will need to be careful here. Once a person is approved for such a role in the church it is more difficult to remove him/her. No-one should be included in the team because the leader thinks it would be good for him/her – only because it would be good for the church. The leader needs to pray about each person and not give an authorisation without real peace of heart. Otherwise, just wait and if pressed, say that the Lord does not yet seem to have given permission.

Importance of Small Groups

The foundation training often starts as we learn to pray for each other in small groups. A sympathetic group is the place where we may learn to invite the Holy Spirit to come, and also to pray aloud which some Christians find very difficult. Breaking the group into smaller cells of three to pray for each other's needs during the last 10–15 minutes may be a great help in building confidence.

Healing Ministry Training

The outline of these training days is given on page 42 and in a separate booklet covering the training. This day is open to those wanting to be part of the New Wine Ministry Team as well as to members from other churches who are welcome, provided they obtain their minister's approval.

Authorization and Follow-up

Provided the individual is already a regular member of the fellowship, belongs to a Home Group, is perceived as stable and willing to accept correction, then after this training and a review by the staff group, he or she may be 'authorised' by the minister to join the Healing Ministry team as a trainee.

The kind of person the minister looks for to include in his/her healing team is:–

1. A converted person who is godly and is open to the on-going ministry of the Holy Spirit in his/her life and has experienced the filling of the Holy Spirit.

2. A person who is committed to the Body of Christ.

3. A person who is teachable.

4. A person who relates well to others.

5. A person who has plenty of common sense.

6. A person who has already invested in the Church (time, energy, money).

A trainee member could have a different coloured ministry badge and work alongside a more experienced member for two or three months before being fully authorised to work with anyone. The individual could then be allowed to minister on his/her own should the pressure of ministry require this, but not in the trainee stage.

Regular training and feedback sessions should be given in the initial stages to groups of trainees, and in the longer term to the ministry team as a whole, through occasional Saturday mornings for feed-back and prayer.

The Guidelines and Practices for the Healing Ministry are given on pages 21–26.

Discipline

Should any report of concern come back to the leader overseeing the ministry team on duty either from someone who has been prayed with or by someone who has prayed alongside an individual, then it should be dealt with straight away if there is something definite on which to act.

If appropriate, our concern should be explained to the particular member of the ministry team and his/her co-operation sought to correct it. It may help to place such an individual with a more experienced member for a few weeks to overcome any difficulty.

We all need to be subject to correction and understand the values in ministry which we hold. It is mainly a departure from these values which causes concern.

If, after some weeks, the individual seems unable to correct the practice or behaviour, or perhaps is having problems in his/her own life, then the situation will be reviewed. The individual will be seen by the minister and if necessary taken off the ministry team for a time. We must be ready to face the discipline if we wish the ministry to have integrity and the church maintain its reputation as a safe place. Some people have a particular problem about accepting correction and if this is known beforehand, they should not be appointed to the team until it is clear that the problem is resolved.

Pastoral Prayer Ministry Training

For those seeking to go on to be involved in the Pastoral Prayer Ministry, a further day of training is involved.

The Pastoral Prayer Ministry Training Day is open to anyone, provided he/she has his/her minister's approval. The outline for the day is given on page 43.

Many find this training day gives them more understanding in this particular area of healing. This is helpful for all members of the ministry team, whether they go on to become part of the Pastoral Prayer Ministry group or not.

Others, already regular members of the Healing Ministry Team, feel called to be available as part of the team for the Pastoral Prayer Ministry. If they indicate this themselves after the Pastoral Prayer Training Day, then they could be invited to join the group and attend the regular follow up training and feedback sessions mentioned above.

Authorization to Minister

Pairs for the Pastoral Prayer Ministry teams are selected and invited to pray with an individual who has asked for help.

Guidelines and Practices in the Pastoral Prayer Ministry are given on pages 33–36.

In addition to the in-house training, everyone in this group should be encouraged to take further training, such as that available through ACC and CWR, without ever abandoning our values.

Supervision and the Handling of Problems

Any Healing Ministry offered during the after-service prayer time, or at any special healing service should be under the authority and supervision of a member of staff or experienced ministry team member who is on duty at the time by arrangement of the Vicar/Pastor. The individual on duty guides those people seeking help to prayer couples, responds to any special problems while avoiding getting involved with praying him/herself – otherwise he/she will have no time to oversee this ministry.

If any problem arises, the difficulty should be referred to the person on duty so that it can be dealt with, either immediately or later, which ever seems more appropriate.

The Statement of Faith and Practice

A Statement of Faith and Practice which applies to both the Healing Ministry and the Pastoral Prayer Ministry sets down what we are offering and how problems should be dealt with. We must do everything we can to avoid the possibility of sending someone away from ministry confused or hurt.

A copy of the Statement is given on pages 37–38.

The Statement seeks to encourage anyone being prayed for to deal with a problem while the team couple appointed to pray are still with him/her. If the individual is not satisfied by the response from the member of the ministry team, then it should be taken up with the staff member on duty. If he/she is still not satisfied, he/she should take it up with the minister in overall charge.

THE INDIVIDUAL'S NEEDS

The Needs

There are many who seek help without realising where their own responsibility lies and how fellow Christians can help them. Nor do they understand the way through to growth and maturity in Christ.

The Centrality of the Cross

Some hold the view that everything for one's growth and maturity is available through Christ's work on the Cross and all one needs is to appropriate it. There is fundamental truth in this position and there are times when we need to sit before the Lord in private prayer for changes to occur. (Psalm 131:2). However, many find it very difficult to approach the Lord in this way and more difficult to change and grow as Jesus would want us to do, without help.

Waiting for a Miracle

There are others who want a magic wand waved over their problems; or they are looking to God for a miracle without effort on their part. God often acts sovereignly in an individual's life, but at the same time expects us to take responsibility for our own lives.

Accepting Responsibility

Those seeking help must recognise that they have to take responsibility for their lives, be open to the Holy Spirit, be willing to pray themselves and take any appropriate action. They must also recognise the value of support and trust from others in the fellowship. It is a process and can be hard work but very worthwhile.

LEVELS OF NEEDS

God's Initiative

The ways of God in the life of an individual are inscrutable. They can rarely be understood, let alone explained and can never be limited. Every one of us is unique with very different experiences and responses to life. Equally, we respond to God's call on our lives in different ways. However, it helps in this ministry to recognise and evaluate what sort of commitment we are making if we start to offer the Healing Ministry and Pastoral Prayer Ministry. If for no other reason, we need to give broad guidelines to our ministry team.

Cases Requiring One Session

This ministry may take place at an after-service time of prayer, during a small group prayer time or even on a one-to-one basis when a friend comes in to have coffee with you.

The individual may have little awareness of what is coming up through the prompting of the Holy Spirit or he/she may come forward in response to an invitation to prayer with a clear understanding of what needs to be dealt with.

Every individual, even if he/she grows up in a normal loving family, has experienced emotional hurt and conditional love. He or she will have fallen into sin and made wrong choices that need to be dealt with, or traumatic experiences which need healing.

This may happen during a single session prayer time as the Holy Spirit brings the memory of the trauma or sin to mind. It may happen at other times in our Christian walk with the Lord especially soon after our conversion and commitment to Jesus, and will continue if we seek to be open to Him through the Holy Spirit. It is possible to deal with issues on our own but sometimes we need help to bring dark things from the past into the Light.

Cases Requiring Three or Four Sessions

Again, those needing help may come from a family without obvious relational difficulties but there may still be deep emotional pain from the past. The facing and releasing of pain or the dealing with sin and its consequences may require more than one session

The reasons may vary greatly but in some situations pain is suppressed as a way of coping with normal living. Getting to the root of a suppressed problem may take time.

For others, God seems to release healing a little at a time. The process cannot be hurried. Sometimes it may take a number of weeks, and occurs whenever the individual concerned comes up for prayer at the after-service time of ministry even when a different couple from the team are available to give prayer support on each occasion. But God is faithful and will respond whoever is praying with us.

We do not see the 'after-service' ministry as a time of significant dialogue and review of past events. Where this is necessary, the individual may be needing Pastoral Prayer Ministry outside the church service setting.

Prayer team members should be discouraged from suggesting or proposing that any individual needs Pastoral Prayer Ministry. It is better to say at the end of a prayer time, "If that has helped, do feel free to come up for prayer again next week – there will be someone here who will be delighted to pray with you."

Examples may vary from something as traumatic as a single event such as rape, to the ongoing pain of emotionally absent parents.

Cases Likely to Lead to An Extended Period of Prayer

No family is truly normal in God's eyes. However, there are some who have experienced deeper emotional trauma where families are not able to relate openly to each other. Often these seem to be families with secrets. They may be called dysfunctional families. People who have experienced significant hurt, made wrong choices and fallen into sin or experienced trauma over a prolonged period may need longer term help.

Much of this healing can come by belonging to a loving church fellowship where the power of God is manifestly present. At times it is helpful to receive individual ministry from a mature couple.

This process can be longer – perhaps up to 6 months or even a year of weekly ministry. This type of ministry will need a prayer couple with some experience. We must, however, recognise our limitation and not offer what we are unable or unwilling to give. We must also recognise that some experiences which have caused deep emotional trauma may require professional help.

We value professional help and must be ready to advise an individual to seek professional support when this is needed. If we are in any doubt, with the individual's permission, we (with the church leader's approval) talk to his/her own doctor and ask for advice.

Recognising our Limitations

Any church seeking to provide and develop a Healing Ministry and Pastoral Prayer Ministry must recognise the various levels of need.

God is sovereign. He can and does wonderful work through lay people being open to the guidance and power of the Holy Spirit. However, each of us must recognise and accept his/her own level of spiritual maturity and limitation and not offer on-going Prayer Ministry to those where clearly professional help must be the main, if not the only route.

Love, prayer for the 'here and now problems' and support should always be available to any member of the fellowship, but in the early days of Pastoral Prayer Ministry in a church it may be right to offer Prayer Ministry only to the first two categories of need where a single appointment or a few sessions is the right response. As the team gains experience and training, so ministry can be extended to those with longer-term needs.

THE PLACE OF MINISTRY DURING AN EMPOWERING BY THE HOLY SPIRIT

Over the last few years churches have seen sovereign works of God when the Holy Spirit has been especially welcomed and invited to minister to the whole of His people.

This is not a document which seeks to review either ministers' or lay people's responses to such situations. It is right, however, to give brief guidelines on how ministry team members can best be available and to encourage the receiving of this sovereign work of the Holy Spirit by the individuals concerned.

Our same values and guidelines are valid, but the involvement by the ministry member should be reduced in contrast to the situation when the individual comes forward for specific prayer in an after-service ministry time.

Ministry team members will often be ministering on their own in public if it is a time of significant outpouring of the Holy Spirit. In such a glorious situation, we simply bless what God is doing and move on. As far as possible even in this situation, team members should minister to their own sex.

If the ministry seems likely to continue for some time, either because the individual is clearly engaged with the Holy Spirit or manifesting in some way with powerful movements or loud cries, then it will be right for a ministry couple to come alongside and stay praying with the individual.

In all cases, we have to be conscious that the individual may fall down under the power of the Holy Spirit and team members should be prepared to guide, support and help the individual down so that he/she does not fall on anyone else or hurt him/herself.

If you are on your own and are concerned that you may not be able physically to support the person, call on some other member of the congregation nearby to help you.

During these periods of ministry, we are finding that individuals go through very powerful experiences of meeting with God. Such encounters often result in healing, a greater awareness and love for Jesus, repentance over sin and many other things. Often we do not discover the fruit until some time later. God is clearly at work in these times in a very significant and beneficial way.

VALUES IN THE HEALING MINISTRY AND PASTORAL PRAYER MINISTRY

The Authority of the Name of Jesus

We must start by knowing Jesus and, through Him, the Father. In His Name there is authority over the powers of darkness.

The Work of Christ on the Cross

On the cross, Jesus bore our infirmities, our sorrows and our transgressions. It was there that the ultimate victory over Satan was won – therefore the cross must be central in any ministry.

The Work of the Spirit

It is only God who ministers – His timing is perfect – we can't heal anyone. The Holy Spirit is the active agent/representative of the Godhead at work in the world today. He dispenses power to use the gifts the Risen Christ has bestowed upon us. It is His work, not ours. We must be Holy Spirit filled and focused.

The Word of God

All our ministry and practices must be in tune with the Word of God, never in contradiction to the clear teaching of Scripture.

The Body of Christ

We need an ever-deepening relationship in the body of Christ. Ministry should integrate a person, bringing wholeness to the individual and the local Church.

The Growth of the Individual

Growth and maturity for the individual is the goal of ministry. With God's help we are seeking to remove whatever may block this.

Love

Every person is precious to God. We must therefore minister lovingly and sensitively, always seeking to respect the dignity of the individual.

Ref: 'Come Holy Spirit' Ch.10; 'Set My People Free' Ch.3.

GUIDELINES FOR THE HEALING MINISTRY

Introduction

To be part of the Healing Ministry Team, besides being a Christian and filled with the Holy Spirit, individuals are required:

> To be a member of the fellowship and belong to a small group.
> To have attended the Healing Ministry Training Day.
> To accept the values, guidelines and practices for the healing ministry.
> To be authorised by the Vicar and submit to his authority and discipline.
> To attend the healing ministry review meetings.
> To commit to the healing ministry on a regular basis.

Some churches have a rota, some encourage everyone to be available whenever they can, and some combine the latter practice with a commitment for particular Sunday services when they know they will be free to help in this way.

The healing ministry usually takes place at the conclusion of services and celebrations and is overseen by someone authorised by the Vicar. An individual wanting ministry comes forward as a result of his/her own initiative and the prompting of the Holy Spirit (possibly through some revelation from God given out by a person in the congregation and repeated for clarity by the person leading the service).

Guidelines

The ministry is not exercised by individuals on their own. Two minister together and refer to one another in an on-going fashion. Those new to the ministry team should initially minister with someone more experienced. Young people should minister with an adult when praying for someone older. If someone comes up with the individual (i.e. a friend or relative), discourage the friend or relative from holding or touching. Sometimes it is better for them to leave the person with the Ministry Team members. Someone of the same sex as the person prayed for should be in the ministry group.

Introduce yourself and remember to wear your name badge whenever ministering. It is helpful to know the person's name and his/her prayer request and how or why he/she is responding to the Holy Spirit. Keep in mind the autonomy and dignity of the person to whom you are ministering.

Make time and room for God to do His work. Invite the Holy Spirit – "Come Holy Spirit". Individuals coming for the first time need to be told how to receive Him. Encourage the individual to welcome Him and to close his/her eyes. Keep your eyes open to see what the Lord is doing. Lay on hands gently. Wait for Him. Bless and honour what the Lord is doing. Be open to revelations from God and offer them sensitively. Allow plenty of time.

Speak in Jesus' Name, if prompted by the Holy Spirit. Address the power of sickness in Jesus' Name. Tell it to leave or "In Jesus' Name, I speak to the pain and command it to go" or "Be healed in Jesus' Name", etc.

If healing seems to be obstructed, ask the Lord for discernment. If some oppression is discerned, it can often be dealt with by breaking the power of … (fear, for example), or whatever you feel is obstructing, **after** first checking with the person. For example, you may sense that the problem is fear, but the person denies it – so don't press the point. At all times we need to respect the individual.

Never tell someone that he/she has an evil spirit of any kind. This would almost amount to a curse and in any case you could be wrong. Do not try to "exorcise" anyone. Refer anyone who claims to be "possessed" by evil spirits to the leadership.

A person who rests in the Spirit (falls down) can usually still hear/respond. Stay with the person (if possible) and pray quietly in tongues. If there are others still needing prayer, then come back between praying and see how the person is. Most often this is all that is necessary. If you feel God is showing you something, check it out with the person resting in the Spirit before praying into it.

If the person you are ministering to becomes untowardly distressed or noisy, take him/her aside (where practical) to minister out of the public eye. Help him/her to get back to his/her own self control unless it appears that God is at work in some special way.

Be prepared to ask for help from a more experienced member of the Ministry Team. We need to know our limitations.

Do not interfere or try to take over the ministry of other ministry team/group unless requested to do so. Equally do not allow someone from outside to take over the ministry from your team. Politely and firmly ask the outsiders to stand back.

Should the leadership make a general invitation for everyone to minister to others around them, you are authorised to oversee those praying to remind and prompt them to conform to our model, to keep their eyes open and watch what God is doing, etc.

You may also be called upon to minister following a general invitation for the whole congregation to be open to the Holy Spirit. In this situation you will be watching for those who show evidence of the Holy Spirit upon them and you should also feel free to bless whatever God is doing in each individual case.

Stop ministering when it seems that the Holy Spirit has stopped but check by asking the person if he/she is aware of anything unusual. Check also for healing, eg, if the prayer is for hearing, follow with suitable test, ie, block the good ear and speak quietly to the ear which was previously deaf and ask, "Can you hear?"

Conclude the ministry by such gentle and kind words as 'This seems to be as far as we can go for the time being. God bless you and see how you go. Come again if this has been a help."

PRACTICES IN HEALING MINISTRY

Interview

Do you know Jesus? (God also wants to heal unbelievers so lack of faith is not exclusive). How long? Are you part of the fellowship? Do you belong to a Home Group?
What do you want Jesus to do for you?
Where or what is the problem?
Keep dialogue to a minimum – no time for a life history.

Diagnosis

This is sought on both the natural and supernatural plane
Try to listen to what God is saying
Be open to revelations from God
Ask yourself why this person has this condition?
Natural – has he/she contracted a disease or hurt him/herself?
Is the problem supernatural – a bondage, a curse, an affliction?
What is the root cause? – emotional, spiritual or physical?

Ministry

Ask the person needing prayer to stand unless this is physically impossible
Ask the person to keep eyes closed and seek God.
Invite the Holy Spirit – let God lead
Wait (be prepared to wait for some time)
Pray in mind and spirit – listen
Watch with eyes open. Bless what God is doing
Relax – encourage the person to be open – reassure if you sense God
Dialogue with the person being ministered to – Ask what is happening

Look for phenomenological responses – eyelids fluttering – obvious hot patches on face or neck – falling – shaking – located pain – the appearance of agitation or peace – or comments from the person, such as "A picture of my father has suddenly come to my mind", etc.,

Try to ascertain what God is saying through the Spirit.

He may give you some instruction. When ministering healing into a certain area do it with a command such as "Be healed in the name of Jesus".

Do not say "have faith", but rather help the person to take a step of faith where you feel more faith is required.

The ministry always involves the work of the Trinity – Father, Son and Holy Spirit.

Check

Ask the person how he/she feels.

Always minister in love and with compassion.

Never bring the person under condemnation (guilty about sin or lack of faith).

Always give glory to God for every and any improvement/healing.

Final Instructions

Do not tell someone he/she is healed if there are no signs.

Do not instruct anyone to give up medication – that should be the doctor's decision – though the person may choose to do it on his/her initiative, advising the doctor of his/her decision.

Often long-term soaking prayer is needed for inner healing.

Invite the person to come back for more prayer but do not allow counselling to take over.*

It may be necessary to give some scriptural guidance – perhaps there is need for a change in life style or to forgive someone.

Final Results

Immediate and complete healing. Give God the glory!

Delayed healing – it may happen on the way home!

Partial healing – praise God for this and suggest further prayer.

No apparent healing at all – either now or later.

* *You are not authorised to exercise a "counselling" or pastoral prayer ministry. The church may also have a pastoral prayer ministry authorised by the leader but care must be taken not to recommend this to 'outsiders' (visitors) as it will very*

quickly become overloaded. If outsiders think they need further help, instruct them to ask their local church leader to direct them. If they are not church-goers, suggest a local church where they might attend and get help.
A resource list is included in the Pastoral Prayer Ministry booklet.

CELEBRATION OR CONFERENCE MINISTRY TEAM GUIDELINES

Ministry is about co-operating with God – Father, Son and Holy Spirit – under the direction of the leadership. Blessing what God is doing.

GENERAL MINISTRY – when the ministry has already been commenced from the platform.

Often God operates sovereignly – we need to allow God to be God! Do not intrude, but help people focus on the Lord and encourage them to go on receiving ... "The Holy Spirit is on you" ... "Go on receiving" ... "Don't open your eyes" ... "I bless what God is doing."

This approach to ministry applies especially following a general invitation from the front to be open and receive the Holy Spirit.

Wherever possible **minister to the same sex as yourself** but during this type of ministry time you may find yourself ministering to either sex and in most cases you will be ministering on your own, ie you are just blessing what God is doing.

INDIVIDUAL MINISTRY – staying with someone to minister longer.

This is usually called for when an individual comes up for specific prayer – or perhaps during general ministry a person may start to manifest more powerfully and one needs to ask what is happening. In such a case a slightly different ministry may develop.

This ministry should be Christ-centred and Holy Spirit led but your part may be more active. In this more intimate ministry you should try to minister in two's.

1. Ask what the person is seeking from the Lord
2. Listen to the recipient and the Holy Spirit
3. Invite the Holy Spirit to come and lead, guide and encourage
4. Wait – it is God's work, not yours
5. You can ask the person questions ie "What is God doing"
6. If you feel it is right, speak to the condition in Jesus' name
7. Offer any words or thoughts sensitively – recognising that you may be wrong
8. Don't be shocked by anyone's disclosure – be loving and remember our values – confidentiality etc
9. Remember there is a place for expressing feelings.
10. Remember the place of repentance – forgiving and being forgiven.
11. If you have a prophetic word or a picture, pray along those lines, or offer the word in such a way that leaves the person the freedom to weigh it. Never insist that it is a word from God. Remember in all the gifts you could be wrong!

If at any time you recognise you should not be ministering to someone, perhaps because they are a different sex from you, it is your responsibility to stop and call someone else in – don't go on alone.

We are there to make things safe – be watchful – look around. Is there a problem if the person should fall? Never push anyone, but watch for their safety, both as they fall and while they are lying down. Encourage them to stay in the Lord's presence and to go on receiving.

Laying on hands is biblical – for blessing (Mt.19:15), healing (Mk.16:8), healing touch (Mt.8:3). Be sensitive as to where you place your hands.

Help to allay a person's fears of what God will do. "Don't be afraid", "It's OK to receive", "It's OK to express your feelings", "You can stop at any time but try to go with it", "God loves you."

The individual has responsibility for his/her own life. Remember Jesus asked "What do you want me to do?" (Mk.10:51) "Do you want to be healed?" It is often important for the individual **to pray out loud** to the Lord if he/she wants guidance, feels stuck or doesn't know what to do next. Don't accept responsibility for his/her life. Avoid projecting into someone else what God is doing in you.
Let them find out what God is doing in them.

Do not let people become dependent on you – eg do not make appointments with people to pray with them outside the meeting, nor allow people to ask for ministry from certain people. If they request further counsel, encourage them to seek ministry in their home church. This is the Holy Spirit's ministry. The person who ministers is not that significant or important. The only exception to this rule is when we recognise we are out of our depth, eg beyond our experience and need to refer the person to someone else with higher authority and more experience.

Never tell a person they have an evil spirit. Assume initially that it is a hurt being manifested. If an evil spirit begins to manifest make sure you have an experienced person with you and your section leader is aware of the situation. 2–3 people should minister – not a single person and not a crowd. Do not minister late into the night. You can always bind the evil spirit and discuss the situation with your section leader.

Anyone reporting physical or sexual abuse needs sensitive support. If you are on your own, get someone to minister with you. If you are dealing with a past experience, you can deal with it as a deep hurt needing safe expression of feeling, a recognition of where the true responsibility lies (with the abuser) which hopefully will lead on into forgiveness and asking God to heal. Remember this is a process and may take time. Don't force people to go faster than they are able. If abuse is current and continuing, it should be reported to your section leader for specific guidelines (see pages 31 and 32).

Guidelines for offering words – Always be gentle and sensitive and remember our values (see page 20). How would you like to be ministered to in this way?

Fear/Anxiety	Ask God to show the cause
	Speak healing in Jesus' Name
	Ask God to come in and comfort and fill with the love of Jesus.
	Pray for peace in the person.
Coming out	Ask God to come and help
of sin (drink	Ask God to strengthen the will
drugs, sexual	Speak release in the Name of Jesus
involvement)	Give permission to express feelings

You are working under authority – so recognise your limits. Don't intrude when others are ministering unless invited. Be open to correction and guidance. If in doubt, report anyone who you feel is mentally sick, needs deliverance, has current physical or sexual abuse, or any accident where someone has been hurt.

Your personal position – keep short accounts with God and your brothers and sisters. Take care about your personal hygiene and clean fresh breath – carry some clean tissues.

GUIDELINES FOR DEALING WITH CHILD ABUSE

Introduction
Symptoms of emotional, physical and sexual abuse may be suspected or such abuse may be reported to us by a child or young person during healing ministry or sharing.

When we believe a child or young person is "at risk" in the situation he/she describes, we have a moral, if not legal, responsibility to report the case to the local Social Services Department. The following notes give guidelines in the situation. Alongside this responsibility, we will continue to minister to the individual, praying for his/her healing and wholeness.

Guidelines
In the event of a ministry team member knowing that a child is "at risk", it should be reported to a member of the church staff or, if at a conference such as "New Wine" or "Soul Survivor", to the team leader.

The Ministry Team Leader
At the time of reporting, the leader should ask the ministry team member to write down in his/her own handwriting exactly what was said, including any special physical or sexual language used. Include also the child's name and address (registration number at conferences).

NB Handwritten notes can be used as evidence. These should be given to the team leader, who should explain what action may need to be taken as a result.

Check the notes subsequently and state clearly when they were written and when the child's comments were made. Raise any obvious questions with the team member.

Do not discuss the report with the young person. It is not your responsibility to investigate the case.

Following this review, if in your best judgement the child or young person is genuinely "at risk", then, following discussion and confirmation with the child's own minister or youth leader, where possible or appropriate, the Social Services Department local to the child's home should be advised and a copy of the team member's notes should be included.

GUIDELINES FOR PASTORAL PRAYER MINISTRY

Introduction

To become a part of the Pastoral Prayer Ministry team individuals are required:

To be a member of the fellowship and belong to a small group.
To be authorised by the leadership (ie, Vicar).
To be a regular member of the Healing Ministry team and to have completed the training necessary for that.
To have attended the one day seminar on Pastoral Prayer Ministry.
To accept the values and the guidelines of Healing Ministry and Pastoral Prayer Ministry.

Guidelines

Pastoral Prayer Ministry in the church is co-ordinated by the vicar's appointed co-ordinator.

When any request comes to the co-ordinator, an initial interview is arranged to decide whether prayer should be offered and who should see the person wanting ministry.

Newcomers to the church are encouraged initially to get involved in the life of the church, join a home group and attend a course such as "Free to Be" (available from Christian Life Training, 1090 N Batavia Orange CA 92867 USA, Tel 001 714 771 9850, Fax 001 714 771 9849). Planned Prayer sessions are not offered to those being medically treated without reference to the doctor concerned. Prayer support, but not in-depth ministry, may be given to someone undergoing psychotherapy.

Pastoral Prayer is undertaken in two's, either two women or a husband and wife team, or, in the case of a man, it may be two men. Team members are discouraged from praying in partnership with a married member of the opposite sex other than one's spouse for any extended ministry. Praying with members of the opposite sex alone is not approved.

The co-ordinator will see that each praying couple is supervised on a regular basis by appointed supervisors . The supervisor is understood to be part of the confidential group, but not involved in ministry.

Three to four sessions are offered followed by a review, which allows for a termination, a break, a referral or the continuation of the defined period of prayer sessions.

Unless otherwise requested by the leadership, pastoral prayer ministry is only offered to a member of the church, ie, one who has attended for some months and belongs to a home group.

If a praying couple takes on an individual from outside the membership, unless requested by the church leadership, this is seen as outside the authority and supervisory structure of the church. The couple must take personal responsibility for such prayer, but it would be unwise to do this without consulting the co-ordinator.

Use of a prayer room on church premises is encouraged, if possible. (This will need to be booked up ahead of time) but any "safe place" is suitable. Ninety minutes to two hours is the normal time spent with an individual. Ministry after 10 pm is discouraged.

Brief records will be maintained by prayer couples. They will not be copied or held centrally and they will be kept confidential. Every six months there is a review of who is being seen. In this way the overloading of any prayer couple is avoided.

PRACTICES IN PASTORAL PRAYER MINISTRY

Basic Guidelines

Quiet Room – "Do not disturb" sign.
Water – tissues.
Length of session 1–2 hours
4 sessions to start, then review
Harmony between the prayer couple

Exploration Time (listen to God, listen to the person)
Ask:
Presenting Problem
Past history through to present day
Physical condition
Spiritual condition
Listen and watch for:
Thinking
Feelings Expressed
Behaviour Patterns (Choices)
Repetitive Dreams
Body Language
Reflect back

Prayer Time

Pray and welcome the Holy Spirit.
Encourage individual to do the same.
Wait.
Ask: – What is happening? Any pictures, memories, feelings?
Remember that the feelings connect present with past.
Expect God to gift you with gifts of the Spirit.
Offer these gifts humbly – you could be wrong!

Resolutions

Possibilities:
Repentance – confess and ask God to forgive
Forgiveness – to those who have hurt us
Renounce inner vows, irrational beliefs
Deliverance from demonic oppression
Bondages broken to a relative or soul tie in Jesus' Name
Ask Jesus to come and heal
Give plenty of time

Post-Prayer Guidance

Let the individual talk about what has been happening during ministry time
Give help where needed with goals or things to be achieved
Explain about not to go to others for ministry
Be supported by Home Group
Permission to phone if in pain or anxiety.
Give home work (eg Ps 139 or Eph 1:3–11)
Read helpful books
Do something creative: paint, sing, sew, cook, garden, etc.
Two way prayer journal – What God says and does.
Make sure he/she knows date and time of next appointment.

Important: When you next see the individual, make sure they know you accept them anyway.

HEALING MINISTRY AND PASTORAL PRAYER MINISTRY: STATEMENT OF FAITH AND PRACTICE

Pastoral Responsibility

We believe that each Church is responsible for preaching the Gospel which brings salvation and healing to the lost. They are also responsible for providing support and encouragement for the growth and maturity of the believers in their care. For this reason, in addition to teaching and discipleship courses, regular courses in personal growth are offered and specific opportunities are given for anyone also desiring to receive general prayer. Also individual pastoral prayer ministry sessions are offered, although this is a ministry confined to Church members only.

Healing Ministry

A time of Healing Ministry is offered after every service to all who have needs for which they would value prayer. A team trained and authorised by the Vicar offers a ministry which is Christ-focused and Holy Spirit-led. The members of the team are open to see what God is wanting to do for each individual.

This prayer ministry in the Church happens through an invitation to anyone needing prayer to come forward at the end of the service. Each person is prayed for by a member(s) of the team under the supervision of an appointed leader. It is also available within small groups under the group leader.

Should any problem arise in the ministry, individuals are encouraged in the first place to take them up with the couple who are praying with them. If they wish to take it further, then they should talk to whoever is on duty or they may contact a member of the staff direct. We value the individual and would not want anyone to go away confused or hurt by our ministry.

Pastoral Prayer Ministry

Pastoral Prayer Ministry is an on-going prayer ministry for deeper emotional needs which is offered on a planned basis and takes place over a period of several weeks or months. This ministry is available to Church members only.

Pastoral Prayer Ministry is covered by a more formal arrangement. The individual makes a request for prayer and is referred to the co-ordinator of the pastoral prayer ministry who then arranges a review session. If prayer is offered, then the individual is referred to a prayer couple and a number of sessions proposed. The basis of the relationship is set out in a letter from the co-ordinator but is covered also by this overall statement of Faith, Practice and Values. Those who are involved in this ministry are regular members of the Healing Ministry team who have in addition received training for planned prayer ministry, are authorised by the leadership and are supervised on a regular basis. On-going training and follow-up meetings are arranged for this group.

We seek to recognise our own limitations in ministry and, should it be necessary, with the permission of the individual, we would refer for help to others where this is felt appropriate. Occasionally this means referral for professional help. However, no reference is made without the individual's specific permission unless the prayer couple feel that the individual is at personal risk.

Prayer couples are supported by a supervisor who will be included in the confidential group but not involved in the ministry. The individual will be advised in their confirmation letter who the supervisor will be.

As with the Church Healing Ministry, any problem arising should in the first place be taken up with the prayer couple, then the supervisor and/or prayer co-ordinator. If the individual is still not happy with the outcome, then it can be taken up direct with the leadership.

OUTLINE LETTER TO THOSE BEING OFFERED ON-GOING PRAYER

Dear ....

I have now talked to .... and they have agreed to give you some time to pray through what you shared with me.

I suggest that you start with three or four sessions of one and a half hours followed by a review. Could you please telephone .... direct to arrange a first session.

As we have a supervisory arrangement, there will be a supervisor, in this case .... who will be part of the confidential group, although not directly involved in the ministry.

As we believe this prayer is an important part of our Pastoral Care to members of the fellowship, I have enclosed a Statement of Faith and Practice for your information.

May the Lord bless you during this time.

Sincerely

Co-ordinator

BOOK OUTLINES

"Come Holy Spirit" (USA title: "Spiritual Gifts in the Local Church") by David Pytches
There is an urgent need to help churches that want to move forward in renewal by integrating the spiritual gifts into their ministry. This is not a rule book, but a set of guidelines for those who need basic teaching material to adopt or adapt. The power ministry has proved a very positive blessing, but it has not been without problems. Part of the answer has been found in regular teaching and talkbacks. David shares these experiences with the reader and encourages others to move into similar ministry under the leading of the Holy Spirit.

Leadership for New Life" by David Pytches
This book is for leaders with followers, ministers, home group leaders, worship leaders – who wish to break new ground for the Kingdom of God and for every church where mission is central.

David shares from his own experience his vision of equipping the saints for God's work. He offers both spiritual and practical advice on virtually every topic relating to leadership and draws on some of the most valuable ideas from other leaders.

"Set My People Free" by Mary Pytches
Mary writes as a lay person engaged in bringing healing to the emotionally damaged. Her conviction – that God intends all of us to be whole – inspires her ministry of inner healing. There is practical help here for ordinary Christians seeking wholeness for themselves and for other people.

"Yesterday's Child" by Mary Pytches
The author lifts the veil from the foundational years of childhood, showing how early experiences have a crucial influence on our adult lives. The reader is taken through the growing process from the pre-natal months into adolescence. Practical exercises suggest ways to move forward into a positive and healing self-awareness.

"A Child No More" by Mary Pytches
Inner childhood hurts must be faced and dealt with if we are to be transformed into the likeness of Christ. This book enlarges the subject matter of "Yesterday's Child" so that the healing experience is seen in the context of Christian growth into spiritual maturity. Mary suggests both individual and group disciplines to help in the process of transformation.

"Dying to Change" by Mary Pytches

Insecurity and low self-esteem can cause many problems in our lives. Difficult feelings and self-protective behaviour patterns often follow and become barriers to maturity. Change is essential if we are to become the people God created us to be but how can this be achieved? The book looks at how even the most vulnerable areas of our lives can be turned round if we learn to remain open to God's transforming power.

"Who am I?" by Mary Pytches

Mary explains that the view we hold of ourselves can often be so distorted as to impair our lives. Am I what culture dictates? Am I what others say about me? Am I what I do? Am I what I look like? Who am I?

This is a practical and enthralling book that guides us through the many levels and depths of our identities – Each chapter includes simple exercises with which to apply the teaching to our lives and find our true identity in Christ.

"Healing Ministry" Training by David Pytches

The training booklet for the day training led by David Pytches in which the biblical background is given for the ministry together with guidelines and a model for ministry. The teaching also includes training for healing the oppressed. The training day is also available on audio and video from Kingdom Power Trust.

"Pastoral Prayer Ministry" Training by Mary Pytches & Prue Bedwell

This training booklet sets out the causes of emotional damage and the consequences in our present lives. The teaching gives the opportunity for self-assessment, details the values which undergird the ministry and provides a model of ministry. This training day is also available on video from Kingdom Power Trust.

HEALING MINISTRY TRAINING DAYS

Purpose: Equipping lay people to minister in the power
                       of the Holy Spirit by:

Content: (a) Teaching
                       (b) Modelling in Ministry
                       (c) Question Time
                       (d) Ministry Time

Day & Time: Saturday, 9 am to 5 pm

Refreshments: Tea and coffee provided
                       Please bring your own lunch

Number: There is no limit to numbers, but prior
                       application should be made and each person
                       coming recommended by their Minister.

Contribution: Each applicant is asked to contribute
                       £10 towards the cost of the day.

PROGRAMME

9.00 am	*Registration*
9.15	*Welcome and worship*
9.30	*Teaching and Ministry (1)*
	"Kingdom and Commission"
10.45	*Coffee Break*
11.15	*Teaching and Ministry (2)*
	"Power and Authority"
	how we minister – model
12.30 pm	*Lunch Break*
1.45	*Teaching and Ministry (3)*
	"Healing the Oppressed"
3.00	*Tea Break*
3.30	*Teaching and Ministry (4)*
	"Values"
5.00	*Finish*

For application details contact Hazel Waterer, 17 Rendlesham Way, Chorleywood
WD3 5HS. Tel/Fax: 01923 350339

PASTORAL PRAYER MINISTRY TRAINING DAY

CONTENT: Teaching on:

(a) Basic ministry skills
(b) A pattern for prayer ministry
(c) The origins of emotional damage
(d) The results of emotional damage
(e) The values which undergird the ministry

Group work

Question time

Ministry time

DAY: SATURDAY

TIME: 9 am to 5 pm

REFRESHMENTS: Tea and coffee will be provided
Please bring your own luncH

NUMBER: There is no limit to numbers but prior application
should be made and each person coming
recommended by their minister/pastor.

CONTRIBUTION: Each applicant is asked to contribute £10 towards the
day's costs.

PROGRAMME: *9.00 am*   *Registration*
9.15   *Worship*
9.30   *Teaching (1) Causes of Emotional Damage*
11.00   *Coffee*
11.20   *Teaching (2) Results of being raised in a
Dysfunctional Family*
1.00 pm   *Lunch*
1.50   *Worship*
2.00   *Teaching (3) Know Yourself, Model of
Ministry*
3.40   *Tea*
4.00   *Teaching & Ministry (4) "Values"*
5.00   *Finish*

*For application details contact Hazel Waterer, 17 Rendlesham Way, Chorleywood
WD3 5HS. Tel/Fax: 01923 350339*

NEW WINE

NEW WINE VISION

Our vision at New Wine is to focus on what the Holy Spirit is doing and saying to the Church today.

NEW WINE MISSION - So we seek:

- To exult the Lord Jesus Christ and to extend His Kingdom
- To listen to what God is saying through His Word and put it into action
- To co-operate with the Holy Spirit in envisioning the Church
- To prepare for Revival
- To model worship which is passionate, intimate, reverent and biblical
- To empower the people of God to move in the Gifts of the Spirit
- To encourage church planting
- To discern where the Spirit is leading in the areas of social responsibility, justice, the community and the environment
- To network with like-minded leaders across the nation
- We will endeavour to carry out this mission from the New Wine office by organising conferences and regional events, through our tapes, albums and videos, our New Wine magazine and a national New Wine network
- We will endeavour to do the same for young people through Soul Survivor.

NEW WINE ACTIVITIES

Annual family and young people's conferences are held during August in Somerset, UK. In addition, training days, leaders days, leaders retreats, one-day conferences and regional events are held throughout the year. Conference booking forms and more information on our leaders' programme are available from:

New Wine
4A Ridley Avenue
Ealing
London W13 9XW
Telephone/fax 0208 567 6717
Web Site www.new-wine.org

For details of Soul Survivor activities for youth call the Soul Survivor office:
Tel. 01923 333331 Fax. 01923 333334
Email info@soulsurvivor.com   Web Site www.soulsurvivor.com